SUICIDE

.

SUICIDE

SOME THINGS WE KNOW, AND SOME WE DO NOT

M. RUSSELL BALLARD

Deseret Book Company
Salt Lake City, Utah

"Suicide: Some Things We Know, and Some We Do Not"
appeared in the *Ensign*, October 1987.

Cover photograph by Craig Dimond
© The Church of Jesus Christ of Latter-day Saints
Used by permission.

ISBN 0-87579-766-0

Printed in the United States of America

10   9   8   7   6   5   4   3   2   1

I RECALL ATTENDING the funeral of an older man who had unfortunately taken his life. His wife had died years earlier, and as his health declined, he felt he had less and less of a reason to live. Gradually he found himself confined to the four walls of his home. A semi-invalid, he was unable to visit friends or go grocery shopping. His food was delivered to his door. He missed going to church, missed regular fellowship with other members of his priesthood quorum.

Although he wasn't able to get about, the doctor assured him he could live many more years. "You neither smoke nor drink," the doctor said. "You've taken good care of yourself. Other than the fact that you're confined to your house and wheelchair, I give you a clean bill of health."

While the doctor was trying to be encouraging, the man felt discouraged. This good brother felt his earthly life no longer had any value, and he wanted to join his beloved wife in the spirit world. The more he thought about death, the more appealing it became to him. He had been a faithful member of the Church all his life; he had served two missions and had been diligent in several leadership positions at different times in his life. But as he thought about the release he would find through death, his mind became muddled. He unwisely concluded that taking his own life would solve his problems.

I visited with the family after the funeral. As you might expect, they were greatly disturbed by what their father and grandfather had done. Their feelings ranged from grief to anger to guilt.

"I should have noticed how depressed he was," one daughter said. "Then I could have helped him and prevented this."

One son spoke rather harshly. "I never thought my father was a stupid man. But what do you say to this? If he loved us, he would never have done such a thing!"

A comment by the youngest son captured the despair they all felt: "There is no hope for Dad now, is there?" he said. It was more a statement than a question. "All the good things he did throughout his life don't matter anymore. Now that he's taken his life, he will be in the telestial kingdom throughout eternity." Then he wept.

The feelings expressed then by those family members are commonly felt by

Latter-day Saints trying to cope with the suicide of a loved one or associate. The anguish and uncertainty they experience are extremely painful and difficult.

Sadly, the problem touches many lives. Every year in the United States alone half a million people try to take their own lives. Fifty thousand of those succeed. Unfortunately, the problem also exists among members of the Church. Consequently, the Church has provided

The act
of taking one's life is truly a
tragedy because this single act
leaves so many victims:
first the one who dies, then the
dozens of others—family and
friends—who are left behind,
some to face years of deep pain
and confusion.

counsel to priesthood leaders in the form of an LDS Social Services booklet entitled *Identification and Prevention of Suicidal Behavior* (stock no. PGSC6178).

The act of taking one's life is truly a tragedy because this single act leaves so many victims: first the one who dies, then the dozens of others—family and friends—who are left behind, some to face years of deep pain and confusion. The living victims struggle, often desper-

ately, with difficult emotions. In addi-
tion to the feelings of grief, anger, guilt,
and rejection which the victims in such a
family feel, Latter-day Saints carry an
additional burden. The purpose of our
mortal lives, we know, is to prove ourselves, to eventually return to live in the
celestial kingdom. One who commits
suicide closes the door on all that, some
have thought, consigning himself to the
telestial kingdom.

Or does he? What *is* the truth regarding suicide?

The prophets have taught us some important principles about suicide, but it is possible that many of us have misunderstood. Let's review some of the fundamental teachings of the prophets on this matter.

First, President George Q. Cannon of the First Presidency made a clear statement about the seriousness of suicide

when he said: "Man did not create himself. He did not furnish his spirit with a
human dwelling place. It is God who
created man, both body and spirit. Man
has no right, therefore, to destroy that
which he had no agency in creating.
They who do so are guilty of murder,
self-murder it is true; but they are no
more justified in killing themselves than
they are in killing others. *What difference
of punishment there is for the two crimes, I*

do not know; but it is clear that no one can destroy so precious a gift as that of life without incurring a severe penalty." (Gospel Truth, 2 vols., Salt Lake City: Deseret Book Company, 1974, 1:30; italics added.)

President Spencer W. Kimball made an equally strong statement in 1976. "It is a terrible criminal act for a person to go out and shorten his life by suicide," he said. (_Teachings of Spencer W. Kimball,_ ed. Edward L. Kimball, Salt Lake City: Bookcraft, 1982, p. 187.)

Those statements on their own might seem to leave no room for hope. However, although they stress the seriousness of suicide, the statements do not mention the final destination of those who take their own lives.

The late Elder Bruce R. McConkie, formerly of the Quorum of the Twelve, expressed what many Church leaders

have taught: "*Suicide* consists in the vol-
untary and intentional taking of one's
own life, *particularly where the person
involved is accountable and has a sound
mind. . . . Persons subject to great stresses
may lose control of themselves and become
mentally clouded to the point that they are no
longer accountable for their acts. Such are
not to be condemned for taking their own
lives.* It should also be remembered that
judgment is the Lord's; he knows the

It should
also be remembered
that judgment is the Lord's;
he knows the thoughts, intents,
and abilities of men;
and he in his infinite wisdom
will make all things right
in due course."

—Bruce R. McConkie

thoughts, intents, and abilities of men; and he in his infinite wisdom will make all things right in due course." (*Mormon Doctrine*, 2d ed., Salt Lake City: Bookcraft, 1966, p. 771; some italics added.)

Not long ago I was asked to speak at the funeral of a dear friend who had committed suicide. Knowing the person and the circumstances as I did, and researching the doctrine on the subject, I had some difficult moments in preparing for my remarks. I know that any fully rational person who contemplates suicide must realize what a terribly selfish act this is. Peace came to me only when I recognized that only the Lord could administer fair judgment. He alone had all the facts, and only He would know the intent of the heart of my friend. I was reconciled with the idea that a lifetime of goodness and service to others must surely be considered by the Lord in judging the life of a person. In the Lord's mercy, perhaps the words of Alma will apply:

"The plan of restoration is requisite with the justice of God; for it is requisite that all things should be restored to their proper order. Behold, it is requisite and just, according to the power and resurrection of Christ, that the soul of man should be restored to its body, and that

And it is
requisite with the justice of God
that men should be judged according to their works; and if their
works were good in this life, and
the desires of their hearts were
good, that they should also, at the
last day, be restored unto that
which is good."

—Alma 41:2–3

every part of the body should be restored to itself.

"And it is requisite with the justice
of God that men should be judged according to their works; and if their
works were good in this life, and the desires of their hearts were good, that they
should also, at the last day, be restored
unto that which is good." (Alma 41:2–3.)

I feel that judgment for sin is not always as cut-and-dried as some of us

seem to think. The Lord said, "Thou shalt not kill." Does that mean that every person who kills will be condemned, no matter the circumstances? Civil law recognizes that there are gradations in this matter—from accidental manslaughter to self-defense to first-degree murder. I feel that the Lord also recognizes differences in intent and circumstances: Was the person who took his life mentally ill? Was he or she so deeply depressed as to be unbalanced or otherwise emotionally disturbed? Was the suicide a tragic, pitiful call for help that went unheeded too long or progressed faster than the victim intended? Did he or she somehow not understand the seriousness of the act? Was he or she suffering from a chemical imbalance that led to despair and a loss of self-control?

Obviously, we do not know the full circumstances surrounding every suicide.

Obviously,
we do not know
the full circumstances
surrounding every suicide.
Only the Lord knows
all the details, and he it is
who will judge our actions
here on earth.

Only the Lord knows all the details, and he it is who will judge our actions here on earth.

When he does judge us, I feel he will take all things into consideration: our genetic and chemical makeup, our mental state, our intellectual capacity, the teachings we have received, the traditions of our fathers, our health, and so forth.

We learn in the scriptures that the blood of Christ will atone for the sins of men "who have died not knowing the will of God concerning them, or who have ignorantly sinned." (Mosiah 3:11.)

Thus, a person who has never heard of the Word of Wisdom, for example, and who becomes an alcoholic will be judged differently from one who knows the Word of Wisdom, *and understands it*, and then chooses the course that leads to alcoholism.

President Kimball's *The Miracle of*

Forgiveness gives us insight into the accountability of some who commit suicide. "A minister acquaintance of mine, whom I knew rather well, was found by his wife hanging in the attic from the rafters," President Kimball wrote. "His thoughts had taken his life. He had become morose and despondent for two or more years. Certainly he had not come to suicide in a moment, for he had been a happy, pleasant person as I had known him. It must have been a long decline, ever steeper, *controllable by him at first and perhaps out of hand as he neared the end of the trail.* No one in his 'right mind,' and especially if he has an understanding of the gospel, will permit himself to arrive at this 'point of no return.' " (*The Miracle of Forgiveness*, Salt Lake City: Bookcraft, 1969, p. 106; italics added.)

Thankfully, the Prophet Joseph Smith taught this enlightening doctrine:

"While one portion of the human race is judging and condemning the other without mercy, the Great Parent of the universe looks upon the whole of the human family with a fatherly care and paternal regard. . . . He is a wise Lawgiver, and will judge all men, not according to the narrow, contracted notions of men, but, 'according to the deeds

While

one portion of the human race

is judging and condemning the

other without mercy,

the Great Parent of the universe

looks upon the whole

of the human family

with a fatherly care and

paternal regard."

—Joseph Smith

done in the body whether they be good or evil,' or whether these deeds were done in England, America, Spain, Turkey, or India. . . . We need not doubt the wisdom and intelligence of the Great Jehovah; He will award judgment or mercy to all nations according to their several deserts, their means of obtaining intelligence, the laws by which they are governed, the facilities afforded them of obtaining correct information, and His inscrutable designs in relation to the human family; and when the designs of God shall be made manifest, and the curtain of futurity be withdrawn, we shall all of us eventually have to confess that the Judge of all the earth has done right." (*Teachings of the Prophet Joseph Smith,* sel. Joseph Fielding Smith, Salt Lake City: Deseret Book Company, 1976, p. 218.)

I draw an important conclusion from

Suicide
is a sin—a very grievous one,
yet the Lord will not judge the
person who commits that sin
strictly by the act itself.
The Lord will look at that person's
circumstances and the degree
of his accountability at the
time of the act.

the words of the Prophet: Suicide is a sin—a very grievous one, yet the Lord will not judge the person who commits that sin strictly by the act itself. The Lord will look at that person's circumstances and the degree of his accountability at the time of the act. Of course, this gives us no reason to excuse ourselves in committing sins, nor will the Lord excuse us, if I understand correctly. We must constantly strive to do our best in emulating the Savior in every aspect of our lives. At the same time, however, let us remember that spiritual growth comes "line upon line," that the key—in the spirit world as well as in mortality—is to keep progressing along the right path.

I recently heard some experiences of families of suicide victims that give hope to others who are suffering. I must point out that individual spiritual experiences of Church members do not determine

Church doctrine. Still, these experiences are compatible with the ideas we have been discussing. The first experience deals with a young woman whose father took his life when she was five years old. The father was not a member of the Church, nor was the daughter until many years later.

"As I was growing up," she relates, "I had the subtle feeling that there was something he very much wanted me to do for him. I had been taught in my church that he had murdered himself and was in hell. But it seemed to me that even though he had been wrong to kill himself, he had thought he was doing the family a favor. (He was an alcoholic who couldn't shake the habit.) I began to search the Bible to see what might have happened to him. As time went by, I came to know that he had somehow suffered through his problems—and that now he needed me to do something for him. I kept thinking, 'But what can you do for someone who is already dead?' And the answer would come, 'Someday, if you keep searching, you will know.'

"Eventually I was baptized into the Church and went to Ricks College. When I first heard of baptism for the dead, I was overwhelmed. Now I knew what my father wanted me to do! I did the necessary work and sent his name to the Idaho Falls Temple, where I had the privilege of seeing a brother baptized by proxy for my father. His endowment work was done the same month. I have a strong feeling that he has accepted both ordinances and is greatly blessed by it."

This next experience was shared by a member of the Church whose father took his life after an extended period of illness. The references to recent discoveries by medical science are enlightening.

"I will never forget calling home that morning in 1977 and having a police lieutenant answer, informing me of my father's suicide. My father was a sweet, kind man who never intentionally hurt anyone. He always thought his body was a temple. Yet something had become wrong with Dad's body, and he had been a very sick man.

———

"Then, in 1980, I experienced a terrible physical change in myself that gave me some insight into my father's state of mind during the weeks preceding his death. I was diagnosed as having hyperthyroidism. My body went through many of the traumas that Dad experienced. I spent a four-month period without sleep. Sleeping pills gave no relief. If I did fall asleep, I awoke soon after, soaked in perspiration. Many of the symptoms were emotional ones. I was frightened and suffered a deep depression. For a year and a half I received medication, and the disease was finally brought under control. I am thankful that I had a doctor who could help me.

"Living through my experience helped me to understand my father's death better. I spent hours doing research and found that little data on hyperthyroidism could be found before 1979.

Thyroid disease can be hereditary, and since my experience, we have discovered it in two of my cousins on my father's side. I also found an article by a doctor who wondered how many people have been in mental institutions with chemical imbalances that could have been corrected.

"Maybe Dad had this same disease. With everything I've studied, I choose to think he did. It helps me deal with his

Dad
believed in the Lord
with all his heart and had
a strong, solid testimony.
His cause of death may have
marred his entrance
into the spirit world,
but not the beautiful life
he had led for
fifty years."

death. For a man who took such good care of himself to fail so fast and become ill so quickly makes me believe he had an undiscovered disease.

"Dad believed in the Lord with all his heart and had a strong, solid testimony. His cause of death may have marred his entrance into the spirit world, but not the beautiful life he had led for fifty years.

"I know my Heavenly Father loves

me and watches over me and gives me the peace I now enjoy."

This next and last experience testifies of the peace that our Father in Heaven can give to those left behind:

"At the time of my mother's suicide, she had lost her earthly companion, was in ill health, and did not accept help freely. She had told my aunt that she could cope with the loss of my father or the difficulties she was having with her health, but that she couldn't handle both. That was two days before she died. I believe she considered suicide very soon after my father was killed in an automobile accident. I was concerned enough to discuss the possibility with her doctor, but no action was taken. The reason for this, I believe, is the lack of understanding we have as a society in dealing with these types of problems.

"I believe the Lord will consider each

I *believe*
the Lord will consider
each case separately
and judge
the circumstances
of each
individual."

case separately and judge the circumstances of each individual. I have sincerely sought direction from our Father in Heaven to help me understand the nature of suicide. And I have come to know, as well as anything else that I know from God, that these people have a place in the kingdom of our Father, and it is not one of darkness or despair, but one where they can receive comfort and experience serenity."

We cannot measure these particular spiritual experiences, of course. We do not know the extent to which the door is open for these particular people to grow and develop in righteousness until they possibly receive the blessings of exaltation. They committed a very serious sin, and some consequences of it may remain with them throughout eternity. Only our Father in Heaven knows the full answer

Only
our Father in Heaven
knows the full answer
to the questions
our hearts ask regarding
those who take their
own lives.

to the questions our hearts ask regarding those who take their own lives.

But it is clear that hope exists. President Joseph F. Smith learned this important principle near the end of a long life of service to the Church. In vision he saw the work of salvation proceeding among the dead, and wrote:

"I beheld that the faithful elders of this dispensation, when they depart from mortal life, continue their labors in the preaching of the gospel of repentance and redemption, through the sacrifice of the Only Begotten Son of God, among those who are in darkness and *under the bondage of sin* in the great world of the spirits of the dead.

"The dead *who repent will be redeemed*, through obedience to the ordinances of the house of God,

"And *after they have paid the penalty of their transgressions*, and are washed clean, shall receive a reward according to their works, for they are heirs of salvation." (D&C 138:57–59; italics added.)

I am grateful for the great plan of salvation our Father in Heaven has provided for us. It is a plan of great fairness and a plan of great love.

As I think about the worry and agony of those whose loved one has taken his or her own life, I find deep comfort and faith in the Lord's promise and

I *am*
grateful for the great
plan of salvation
our Father in Heaven
has provided for us.
It is a plan of great fairness
and a plan of
great love.

blessing to us who remain in mortality: "Peace I leave with you, my peace I give unto you: not as the world giveth, give I unto you. Let not your heart be troubled, neither let it be afraid." (John 14:27.)